A Spiritual Journey

Judith Jennifer

ISBN 979-8-89112-351-9 (Paperback)
ISBN 979-8-89112-352-6 (Digital)

First Edition

Covenant Books
11661 Hwy 707
Murrells Inlet, SC 29576
www.covenantbooks.com

PREFACE

God's love and protection for us are paramount. In return for His ultimate sacrifice, when He died a very painful death, we must love Him above all things. It's written in *Proverbs 3:5–6 (KJV)*, "Trust in the Lord with all thine heart, and lean not unto thine own understanding. In all thy way acknowledge him, and he shall direct your paths."

This world holds nothing for us because, in the end, we are going to succumb to death. There is nothing we can take with us, no matter how much we have accumulated to amuse ourselves with. They are all borrowed from Him. He wants to put a little joy into our lives.

We must remember that God is always working on our behalf, no matter how difficult the journey. When we accept Christ as our Lord and Savior, we will realize that nothing seems arduous. Our eyes are open, and good things start to happen in our lives. Always bear in mind that He is love. We must get to know His name so that all our trust will be in Him. God will never forget those who are humble.

Do you know that the more we get to know Him, the more we will change to be like Him? Our sinful ways will change as we come to have a much deeper love and understanding of Him.

In troubled times, we must call upon him, but we must do so not only then but continuously; this way, He will guide us according to our circumstances. Therefore, spending time in prayer is a good start. Sometimes, it is difficult to begin. In *Romans 8:26 (KJV)*, it says, "Likewise the Spirit also helps in our weakness. For we do not know what we should pray for as we ought, but the Spirit Himself makes intercession for us with groaning which cannot be uttered."

In prayer, we can feel His presence. Here, we can see how wonderful He is. There will be times when our requested prayers are not answered, as we think they should be. God knows what is best for us. Nevertheless, He is beside us. Remember that our salvation manifests in the righteousness of God. We must allow the Spirit to channel through.

Yes. We are all sinners. This fact is true. So in saying that we accept God, we have to be willing to change our hearts. We must obey all His laws while walking on the right path. This is when grace intercedes. David reminds us all. What a wonderful feeling that is! "Oh, how love I thy law! It is my meditation all day" (*Psalm 119:97).*

God has given us free will; therefore, He would like us to get to know Him willingly. He will never force us, but He would like to carry out His plan of salvation that He has for us. He wants us to worship Him and glorify Him by how we live our lives while keeping faith and staying obedient. When we place our faith in Jesus Christ, we become God's family.

SCRIPTURES

> Now therefore ye are no more strangers and foreigners, but fellow citizens with the saints, and of the household of God; And are built upon the foundation of the apostles and prophets, Jesus Christ himself being the chief cornerstone; In whom all the buildings fitly framed together groweth unto an holy temple in the Lord: in whom ye also are builded together for an habitation of God through the spirit. *(Ephesians 2:19–22 KJV)*

> For I know the thoughts I think toward you, saith the Lord, thoughts of peace, and not of evil, to give you an expected end. (*Jeremiah 29:11*)

I wrote this book for anyone who is going through difficult times. I can attest that I have had a few rough patches in my life. I grew up in a household where it was mandatory to attend church and Sunday school, but after that, I don't remember picking up the Bible and reading about all the good things it has in store. I wish I had come to know the Lord sooner in my life instead of walking in my own way most of the time.

I am so elated that I found Jesus Christ, and He is the center of my universe. I know that I am grounded in my unshakable faith, and I strongly rely on the Lord to guide me as I move about on my daily journey.

My hope for this book is that it will help anyone who is discouraged or is finding it hard to focus because the things in this world are consuming them. I pray that you find peace, joy, love, faith, and grace as you give your life to Christ by becoming anew in His presence.

Thank you, dear readers, for joining me on this journey. I really do appreciate your support. I would also encourage each one of you to continue exploring your faith.

May God's gracious blessing be upon anyone who finds the time to read my book. It is filled with scriptures, prayers, poetry, a few stories, and a bit of humor.

I just want to say thanks in advance. God loves you so much. Bountiful blessings!

A PRAYER OF THANKS

Dear God,

Thank You for each day that You give me breath. No matter what the season, I embrace it with my whole heart. At times when the struggle is real, I wonder if I will ever get through it, but it is always wonderful to know that You are holding me up.

I don't know what plans You have for me, but I eagerly await them. Lord, Your mercies endureth forever (*Psalm 136* KJV).

It seems like we are living through the end of time. Everything is happening so fast. I can't keep up. I must always remember that great is Thy faithfulness, as You give me mercy moment by moment. I have suffered heartache and the loss of family and friends, but I know that Your mercy and grace are stronger than my loss.

I have learned to depend on You only for love and strength. And as long as I have You, I am not broken.

Yes, sometimes I feel the sting, but my dependence on You and Your love for me is what holds me together. You are my glue, Lord! My plan for my life is to follow the path that You have already mapped out for me.

Thank You for always being with me, and I am so glad that You never change, unlike man whose emotions are so fickle.

Amen.

SCRIPTURES FOR CALM DURING THE TEMPEST

Cast thy burden upon the Lord, and he shall sustain thee: he shall never suffer the righteous to be removed. (*Psalm 55:22 KJV)*

Humble yourselves therefore under the mighty hand of God, that he may exalt you in due time. (*1 Peter 5:6 KJV*)

And even to your old age, I am He. And even to gray hairs I will carry you! I have made, and I will bear: Even I will carry, and will deliver you. (*Isaiah 46:4 KJV)*

He shall feed his flock like a shepherd: He shall gather the lambs with his arm, and carry them in his bosom, and shall gently lead those that are with young. *(Isaiah 40:11 KJV)*

Bear ye one another's burden, and so fulfill the law of Christ. (*Galatians 6:2 KJV)*

COMFORT DURING THE TEMPEST

When my husband decided he wanted out of our marriage because of a misunderstanding, it devastated me. This was the person I saw myself with in my twilight years and at the end of my life, but now it was unraveling. I remember telling everyone that I was alright with the decision that he made, but I realized that I was lying to myself. It was harder than I anticipated, especially coming to terms with a divorce.

They never saw the tears I shed when I got up suddenly every morning at four. Then I could not talk with him because he stopped communicating with me. All texts and communications were ignored. My heart was broken.

I first met my husband forty years ago, when we were both in our twenties. We dated for a while and even talked about getting married. I thought he was the most altruistic person I had ever met. Since both of us were young, life got in the way. So we drifted apart and went on to live different lives. During those years, I never really knew what happened to him, but I did hear he got married, and I remember feeling a little uncomfortable about that bit of news. I came to terms with it.

Faith brought us back together, and we connected forty years later. Speaking of being in the wilderness, I never hesitated as I jumped back into a relationship with him. By now, I had a beautiful daughter and two wonderful grandchildren. These beautiful babies have given me the opportunity to do things differently, as they bring out the joy in me. Soon, my husband and I decided that we should get married, and as you can imagine, it was also one of the happiest moments of my life.

Although I lived in another state and he lived in New York, he assured me that it would not be a problem. I visited him, and he would also visit me. I never wanted to live in New York again. The cold weather was too much for me. Also, the hectic pace wasn't for me anymore. So my heart was at ease when he told me that after he retired, he would join me. I had nothing to worry about.

During our almost five years of marriage, we did have our differences. The distance was hard, but we wanted to make it work, and we did try. It would have been great to have companionship during my twilight years.

After the incident, he wanted out. I saw my life in slow motion. He had cut me off completely. Nevertheless, through all my sleepless nights and my nervous stomach, my faith in God never wavered. There were times when I thought I would burst from anxiety, but God was there for me, comforting me through it all. I felt His presence.

My divorce papers came in November, exactly twelve days before our fifth anniversary. Ouch! It's now been nine months since I last heard my husband's voice. He had removed himself completely from me. I also prayed that I would, but then I knew that wasn't God's plan.

One morning, while I was deep in prayer, a calm peace came over me; it was something that I had never felt before. I heard a voice telling me it would be alright. I thought at first my mind was playing tricks on me, but then I heard the gentle whisper again. In the midst of my despair, God intercepted and proved His love for me. I prayed harder than I had before. The tears came too, but not sad ones—joyful ones.

There in the dawn, my heart was lifted. I knew then that if my husband wanted a divorce, I would comply with his wishes. I realized that God had used me for His glory by putting me through trials. *Philippians 4:6* (KJV) says, "Be careful for nothing, but in everything by prayer and supplication with thanksgiving let your request be made known unto God."

I know that He has me. These days, I sleep past 4:00 a.m. God has once again given me a new lease on life. I did go through the fire, but He didn't let me be consumed by it. Although I still cared for my husband, I was able to be at peace with the divorce. I'm not saying that it was easy, but my anchor held as the storm battered against my heart. I had to dig deeper and lean heavily on the support of my Lord, asking for strength as I worked around and through the pain I was struggling with. The Lord stayed and walked me through it. He held me up. The Bible became my constant companion, along with prayer and fasting.

I am so overjoyed that I am still getting to know the words of the Lord on a much deeper level. Now I can think fondly about my husband, as I reminisce about the good times we had, without the pain. I pray for him and ask God to keep him safe. I do want him to have a blessed life.

The Comforter calms my fears and fills me with hope for the future. As *Isaiah 41:10* (KJV) promises, "Fear thou not, for I am with thee, be not dismayed, for I am God. I will strengthen thee: yea, I will help thee: yea: I will uphold thee with the right hand of my righteousness."

To put our lives back together, we have to get acquainted with His words. We have to get familiar with the Bible. Jesus reminds us that He is the only way to the Father, and we have to live by His teaching. *John 14:6* (KJV) reminds us, "Jesus saith unto him, I am the way, the truth, and the life: no man cometh unto the Father, but by me." As human beings, we will miss the mark sometimes, but we must get back on the straight and narrow. Yes, the tempest will come. Most of the time, it comes without warning. That is why our house should be built on the rock, and that rock is Jesus. He has a very compact structure.

God knew the exact time when He would send His Son to die for us on the cross. He wanted to save us, sinners. What will you do for Him?

Don't wait for the storm to consume your life. Pray before it comes. Believe me, it would be easier to take. Ask yourself if you can withstand the tempest alone or count on Jesus. *Would your anchor hold?*

GOING TO GOD IN PRAYER

When we go to God in prayer, we must go humbly. There is no need to put on airs or come to Him with an ego. People with egos think they are special and superior. All false thinking only leads to lies and alienation. So we must leave all this attitude behind and go meekly. God already knows what brought us to this place. He just wants to hear from you.

In *Matthew 11:28–30* (KJV), it specifically states, "Come unto me, all ye that labour and are heavy laden, and I will give you rest. Take my yoke upon you and learn from me: for I am meek and lowly in heart: and ye shall find rest unto your souls. For my yoke is easy, and my burden is light." It's an invitation to lay all your troubles on Him. If we had faith in Him, our issues would be easier to handle.

Most of us think that prayers should be answered immediately. But if that were true, we would all have what we wanted, but this is not God's plan.

We, as Christians, must put our faith and trust in God at all times. We cannot be fair-weather Christians and only praise Him when things are great with us. He may not give us what we ask for because it may not be the right time. God truly knows what's best for us. *Jeremiah 1:5* (KJV) makes that point: God says, "Before I formed you in the womb, I knew thee; and before thou camest forth out of the womb I sanctified thee, and I ordained you prophet to the nations." I have crossed paths with a few individuals who have difficulty with this verse, but we have to remember that God is the one in control. It took some time for me, too, but I have acknowledged it.

Staying in constant prayer, spending time reading and understanding the Bible, and fasting are ways to get closer to God. Let's see what *Matthew 6:16–18* (KJV) has to say:

> Moreover when we fast, be not, as the hypocrites, of sad countenance: for they disfigure their faces, that they appear unto men too fast. Verily I say unto you, they have their reward. But thou, when thou fastest, anoint thine head, and wash thy face. That thou appear not unto men to fast, but unto thy Father which is in secret: and thy Father, which seeth in secret, shall reward thee openly.

Be sincere about it. As we already know, He sees all.

Just saying that you accept Christ as your personal Savior but continue walking in your willful way is not the intention of God. We, as Christians, have to stay the course. When we become joined to Christ, we must let go of our old ways. It states in *2 Corinthians 5:17* (KJV), "Therefore if any man be in Christ, he is a new creature: old things are passed away, behold, all things become new." This verse is self-explanatory.

Of course, there will be times when life gets in the way. And then, when we try to handle it while leaving God out, things will definitely get messy. But God already knows that will happen. After all, He gives us free will. He still expects us to come to Him and ask for His forgiveness. Spending time with God is part of the course of being a good Christian, and the journey is a long, arduous one, so don't be that person who only stays when things are progressing smoothly. Be the one who continues to praise Him even in the bad times.

For me, after standing in the presence of God, I feel my burdens lifting. It is so wonderful to abide in His love! God's words give me lucidity. Whenever I read them, it lifts my spirit.

So why won't I serve Him for the rest of my life?

Remember, when we pray, we are having a conversation with our Heavenly Father. We must address Him accordingly. As the Bible says, we must all approach Him as our loving father. Again, we must go humbly to Him as we ask for forgiveness while also asking Him to help us resist all the bad influences that are lurking, just waiting to take over our lives.

SCRIPTURES AND WORDS TO LIFT THE SPIRIT

And when thou prayest, thou shalt not be as the hypocrites are: for they love to pray standing in the synagogues and in the corner of the street, that they may be seen of men. Verily I say unto you, They have their rewards. But thou, when thou prayest, enter into thy closet, and when thou hast shut thy door, pray to thy Father which is in secret; and thy Father which seeth in secret shall reward thee openly. But when ye pray, use not vain repetitions, as the heathen do: for they think they shall be heard for their speaking. Be not ye therefore like unto them: for your Father knoweth what things ye need, before ye ask him. *(Matthew 6:5–8 KJV)*

Confess your faults one to another, and pray one for another, that ye may be healed. The effectual fervent prayer of the righteous man availeth much. *(James 5:16 KJV)*

These things I have spoken unto you, that you might have peace in the World, ye shall have tribulations: but be of good cheer, I have overcome the world. *(John 16:33 KJV)*

> And when I come, whomsoever ye shall approve by your letters, them will I send to bring your liberality unto Jerusalem. *(1 Corinthians 16:3 KJV)*

> For God so loved the world, that he gave his only begotten Son, that whosoever believeth in him should not perish, but have an everlasting life. *(John 3:16(KJV)*

The last scripture above is one of the most powerful ones that are written. God sacrificed His only Son for us, sinners. Who do you know will die for you? Would you do that for anyone? We have to allow God's love to transcend through us, and it begins by allowing ourselves to get closer to God, allowing us to see us as He sees us. "Love the Lord thy God with all thine heart, and with all thy soul, and with all thy might," as *Deuteronomy 6:5* (KJV) reminds us. He wants you to keep seeking His love and compassion consistently.

Jesus knew that He would suffer in the world, but He also knew that He came to give us, sinners, comfort. He is our security blanket. Sometimes, life isn't a bed of roses like some people would like to believe. All Christians have shortcomings. As we navigate this life, there are so many pains and weights we have to bear. It could be physical, spiritual, or emotional. Through it all, we have to keep our focus on God because, when we do, we will be capable of handling the heaviest load. He said in *Matthew 11:28* (KJV), "Come unto me. All ye that labour and are heavy laden, and I will give you rest."

He is always there to listen to our prayer and will sometimes answer it, but even if He doesn't answer, as we expect, He is always there right beside us. Prayer is such a great comfort. He alone knows exactly what's best for us. There is no guesswork with God!

He has sovereignty over every action that we take or are about to take.

Let us all be mindful of what being a good Christian is. It's having a connection with our Lord and Savior, Jesus Christ, and knowing that you will only enter the realms of heaven through forgiveness and the righteousness that is granted by Him. As human beings, we distance ourselves from God, so He had to send His Son to die on the cross and shed His blood for us for the remission of our sins so that we could come back to Him. Because of Jesus, we are living under grace. He will protect us from our disastrous behavior.

What a price he had to pay for our sins!

Remember

Pray earnestly. Stay constantly reading and understanding the Bible. Ask God to lift all the heavy burdens that you can't bear. Don't be afraid to cry out to Him. We find time in our busy schedules to do other things. Find time for Him too. Make God your number-one priority. After all, He died for us all. Keep focus. *Isaiah 53:5* (KJV) says, "But he was wounded for our transgressions: the chastisement of our peace was upon him, and with his stripes we are healed." *Why?* Because He loves us!

NO GREATER LOVE

When God speaks about His love for us, He isn't talking about the love of people who are attracted to each other. The love He is talking about is His fatherly love that He has for us and our love for Him. It's called agape love, which surrounds, protects, and delivers us. It's also unconditional and selfless.

In *John 15:13* (KJV), it states, "Greater love has no one than this: to lay down one's life for a friend." This is a very strong Bible verse. How many people do you know will do that? I don't know of anyone who would. Yet God sent His Son to suffer an excruciating death for us sinners because we needed saving.

We all have to show genuine love and care for each other, as Jesus said that we should. In simple terms, love one another. When we look around, we see God's presence everywhere—from the sky to the grass we walk on, the air that we breathe, the wind, the rain, and so many other things that we take for granted. We hear the birds singing so sweetly in the trees and smell the beautiful flowers, which permeate the atmosphere with their sweetness. To me, all this is the presence of God.

We have to give Him the chance He deserves. He died so that we could live. God wants to restore our severed relationship. He just wants us to atone for our sins. God sent His Son—His name is Jesus—to die for our sins. Take a moment to ponder that statement. Why did Jesus have to pay the ultimate sacrifice for us sinners? Because if he didn't, and if it was left up to us, our miserable lives couldn't be worthy of God.

After Jesus ascended, God still sent the Holy Spirit to live inside us. God didn't send Jesus because we are such wonderful human beings. He sent Him because we are sinners, and to top it off, He still loves us. We certainly don't deserve it. He loves us unlimitedly. It comes with requirements, though. He requires us to study His Word, pray, and fast. Most of what He asks evades us. But God never stopped showing His love for us. We have to improve our love for God daily. God is not looking for perfection because He is the only perfect being.

Do you really know the meaning of unlimited? Let me tell you. It's without restrictions or limits. We must love one another without limits, the same way God loves us. Yes. We are living in a finite world where there are rejections, broken marriages, loud and forceful people, liars, cheaters, backbiters, and lots of failed promises. No wonder it's so difficult to understand God's unlimited love, and He cares so much for us. This is where we have to stay with His Word while staying steadfast in prayer. This way, we foster an ongoing relationship with Him. Make peace with God.

Growing up in the West Indies, I always heard that everything must be earned and that nothing is free. As I grow older, that statement still applies. But I found something free. God's love. It's free! Free! Free! His love for us is not controlled or stopped. He pours it all on His children—us. Not one dime must be paid to receive it. His death lifted that burden. Staying on the course helps us stay connected to Him. There is nothing in life that we have done that we can't seek forgiveness from the Lord.

Look at Saul from Tarsus. He was from a wealthy family, a descendant of the tribe of Benjamin. If you read the Bible, Benjamin was Jacob's and Rachel's pride and joy, along with Joseph, his brother. Saul was a tax collector, one of the most disgraced professions in those times. He was a prosecutor of Christians for calling Jesus a savior. After he was blinded on the road to Damascus by a bright light, he turned his life around and became a Christian when his sight was restored.

Matthew was also a tax collector who was Jewish, but he collected taxes for the Romans. From the moment Jesus called him, he dropped everything and followed Him. Matthew made amends with the people he cheated on and then gave up all his worldly possessions and committed his life to Christ.

There was also Zacchaeus, another tax collector. He repented and changed his life after he heard the preaching of Jesus. Jesus had supper at his house. Zacchaeus changed his life after he saw the compassion that Jesus had for sinners. All these people gave their lives to Christ after living so terribly. They were also forgiven. So I ask, Why not you?

Then there was Samson. Most people know the story of Samson and Delilah, but do you know the story of Samson himself? He was a Nazarite (the last of the major judges who led Israel). He dishonored many rules that the Nazarites held sacred. *Numbers 6* (KJV) lays out a description of the rules that a Nazarene must follow, but it seems as though he broke them all. In most cases, he was acting more like a hoodlum than the leader that he was supposed to be. One could say that he turned his back on God. He never respected or had regard for authority. His atrocities were many.

Then when he had no other place to turn, he cried out to the Lord. In *Judges 16:28* (KJV),

> And Samson called unto the Lord and said, "Lord God, remember me, I pray thee, and strengthen me, I pray thee, only this once, O God, that I may be at once avenged of the Philistines for my two eyes."

The Lord heard his cry and came to his aid.

Friends, as I said before, it does not matter what happened in the past. God forgives, although we must repent. In *1 John 1:8–10* (KJV),

> If we say that we have no sin, we deceive ourselves, and the truth is not in us. If we confess our sins, he is faithful and just to forgive our sins, and to cleanse us from all unrighteousness. If we say that we have not sinned, we make Him a liar, and His word is not in us.

When we become Christians, the pressure mounts. You are scrutinized from all angles. People expect you not to make any mistakes, and then when you do, they are shocked. But as finite beings, God anticipated all our failures. Some people strive for perfection, and when that doesn't happen, they are hard on themselves. We have to remember that God alone is perfect. The difference is that we atone for our sins. Turn to the Bible for your answers.

There are times when others will ridicule you. Family and friends may even desert you. You alone must decide if you continue to follow the pack and walk in a destructive way or get on the straight and narrow. It's so easy to go in the direction of a strong wind, as it pushes you along. Try going up against it, and you will see it's a real struggle. You don't have to run with the pack to fit in unless you are the one leading them on a journey to Christ. He is with you every step of the way. You don't have to fix yourself before going to him; just go as you are. Submit yourself to Him. His arms are wide open. *It's never too late to get back to God.*

PRAYERS FOR CALM

Lord,

I am asking You to keep me focused. Let the things that are going on in the world not keep me away from You. I just want to get closer to You, Lord. Help me stay rooted in my faith so that I never walk in my own willful way.

Help me, Lord, to never stray from my thoughts and keep my tongue from uttering careless words. When things become difficult, please help me not to moan about it and see it as a possibility for things You have stored up for me.

Lord, help me to always live by Your word, and thank You so much for the grace and mercies that You have bestowed on me. Let me always be reminded about the words in *Lamentation 3:22–23* (KJV), which say, "It is of the Lord's mercies that we are consumed, because his compassions fail not. They are new every morning; great is thy faithfulness."

In Your name only,
Amen.

> Remember, O Lord, thy tender mercies and thy loving kindness; for they have been ever of old. Remember not the sins of my youth, nor my transgressions: according to thy mercy. Remember thou me for thy goodness sake, O Lord. *(Psalm 25:6–7 KJV)*

Father,

When my worries consume my being, help me always to feel Your presence surrounding me. When I get choked up with fear, remind me to take each breath gradually.

Lord, when my mind races beyond my rational thoughts, give me a soothing word so that I can stay calm.

Each morning, when you wake me up, my choice is to trust You. I know that because of Your grace and mercies, I am still standing, facing another day.

Thank You for all that You have done to keep me grounded. Thank You for loving this sinner.

"Let the word of my mouth and the meditation of my heart be acceptable in thy sight, O Lord, my strength, and my redeemer" *(Psalm 19:14 KJV).*

This I ask, in Your name.

Amen.

Dear Lord,

Please help me not to worry about anything that I can't control. Remind me that because of Your love for me, You will stay with me as I navigate the rough path so that I should never fear the outcome.

This I ask in Your name.

Amen.

Father,

You are my everything. You are with me when I go and when I come. As I open my eyes today, I want to praise You for bringing me safely through another night.

Help me to exercise patience with others, as You do with us.

When I hear my heartbeat echoing in my ears, please slow me down so that I can concentrate only on You. Help me understand that whatever I am going through, it's just a test to get me closer to Your kingdom. I want to be like Job and never waiver.

Lord, I want to trust You with my whole heart because You know what is best for me. Teach me how to focus on Your directions before I take the wrong path. I want to always stay on the straight and narrow path and not on the wide road of the world, which can only lead to a destructive path.

Remind me, Lord, that even if my life becomes difficult, You are always beside me, helping me along.

It says in *Psalm 34:17–18* (KJV), "The righteous cry, and the Lord heareth, And delivereth them out of all their troubles. The Lord is nigh unto them that are of a broken heart; and saveth such as be of a contrite spirit." Help me to always remember this reality.

Lord, I ask this in Your name only.

Amen.

SCRIPTURES FOR CALM (KJV)

Now the God of hope fills you with joy and peace in believing, that ye may abound in hope, through the power of the Holy Ghost. *(Romans 15:13)*

Peace I leave with you, peace I give unto you: not as the world giveth, give I unto you.

Let not your heart be troubled, neither let it be afraid. *(John 14:27)*

I have set the Lord always before me: because he is at my right hand, I shall not be moved. *(Psalm 16:8)*

Trust in the Lord with all thine heart; and lean not unto your own understanding. In all thy ways acknowledge him, and he shall direct thy paths. *(Proverbs 3:5–6)*

Therefore I say unto you, Take no thought for your life, what ye shall eat, or what ye shall drink, nor for your body, what ye shall put on. Is not life more than meat, and the body more than reimnet? Behold the fowl of the air: for they sow not, neither do they reap, nor gather into barns; yet your heavenly Father feedeth them. Are you not much better than they? Which of you by taking thought can add one cubit unto his stature. *(Matthew 6:25–27)*

I will lift up my eyes to the hills-From whence comes my help? My help comes for the Lord. Who made heaven and earth. *(Psalm 121:1–2)*

What shall we say to these things? If God be for us, who can be against us? *(Romans 8:31)*

So that we may boldly say. The Lord is my helper, and I will not fear what man shall do unto me. *(Hebrews 13:6)*

And let the peace of God rule in your hearts, to which also you were called in one body; and be thankful. *(Colossians 3:15)*

ALL THINGS ARE POSSIBLE

Most Christians use this phrase. This is a statement that Jesus made; it is written in *Matthew 19:26* (KJV). It tells us that with His mercy and power, He can do anything. It's a great reminder that with His help and because of His power, we will overcome all things and achieve things that seem beyond our reach.

I hope that we all know that we are at God's mercy. God sees what we are going through, and sometimes He will remedy the situation. Other times, He would stay close to us, as we go through our trials. It's one of the characters that God possesses. He is everywhere, especially when we devote time to Him and make our purpose known. Yes, all things are possible with God. But is it possible to get everything? Imagine if we all got our hearts' desires; this world would be a more catastrophic place than it is now. In *Proverbs 16:8* (KJV), "Better is a little with righteousness than great revenues without right."

He is the only one Who decides what we get in this lifetime. It may be a while before your prayers are answered, or they may be answered immediately or not at all. Don't be dismayed. We, as Christians, must keep the faith. *Hebrews 11:1* (KJV) explains what faith is: "Now faith is the substance of things hoped for, the evidence of things not seen."

When you are seeking that ultimate position that you set your heart on and then it doesn't happen, you are devastated. Your faith may waver a bit, but if you really have faith and hold on to your beliefs, He will always be there for you.

We take the text in the Bible so carelessly. I see people wearing it across their chests as advertisements on T-shirts. I wonder if we are wearing it as a logo or looking for a blessing without putting in the work required.

For most of us, it's a comfort, and it allows us to be encouraged just to know that God is with us. There is nothing wrong with it, but we have to keep our focus, knowing that it's His will. Wearing that sign doesn't change anything. Maybe it makes us feel superhuman. The Lord thy God is much bigger than us, and we can never tell Him what to do.

Jesus asked God to take away the cup while He was being crucified. Just read what it says in *Matthew 26:39* (KJV):

> And he went a little further, and fell on his face, and prayed, saying "O my Father, if it be possible, let this cup pass from me: nevertheless not as I will, but as thou wilt."

Do you remember when he said, "Not my will, Lord, yours"? This was because God's plans were already in play: for Him to die and save us, sinners. It's not because everything is possible with God that He will always intervene. But even when what you desire doesn't happen, as a steadfast Christian, one should feel confident that He is good. He will never leave us alone. He is there right alongside you, guiding you through your troubles.

Examine your own salvation, and then you will find out God cares for you personally, and that is because He knows what plans He has already put in place for you. *Jeremiah 1:5* (KJV) reminds us: "Before I formed thee in the belly I knew thee; and before thou camest forth out of the womb I sanctified thee, and I ordained thee prophets unto nations."

All these revelations wouldn't come overnight, and some may not even acknowledge them, especially when you are hurt and have been passed over for the promotion for which you interviewed many times, only for it to be given to someone else. Questions will surface about not being good enough, and you may even become bitter. But as time progresses, if you stay in prayer, you will realize it was not a good fit for you. So yes, God does answer prayer, and all things are possible with Him. He alone knows what's good for you.

Once we make Him our first priority in everything that we do, He will handle the rest for us. The scripture 2 *Corinthians 4:17–18* (KJV) says,

> But our light afflictions, which is but for a moment, is working for us a far more exceeding and eternal weight of glory, while we do not look at the things which are seen, but the things which are not seen. For the things that are seen are temporary, but the things which are not seen are eternal.

If we realize that He walks with us and He is the one being What knows what is good for us, we will be much better off. God wants us to be holy. We must foster a relationship with Him. We must always come to him humbly, confess our sins, and live according to His Word.

What a friend we have in Jesus!

SCRIPTURES

But Jesus beheld them, and said unto them, with men this is impossible, but with God all things are possible. *(Matthew 19:26 KJV)*

Fear not; for I am with thee, be not dismayed, for I am thy God. I will strengthen thee, yea, I will help thee, yea, I will uphold thee with the right hand of my righteousness. *(Isaiah 41:10 KJV)*

In all your ways acknowledge him, and he shall direct your path. *(Proverbs 3:6 KJV)*

Therefore I say unto you, What things soever ye desire, when ye pray, believe that ye receive them, and ye shall have them. *(Mark 11:24 KJV)*

What shall we then say to these things? If God be for us, who can be against us? *(Romans 8:31 KJV)*

Behold, I am the Lord, the God of all flesh: is there anything too hard for me? *(Jeremiah 32:27 KJV)*

In all thy ways acknowledge him, and he shall direct thy paths. *(Proverbs 3:6 KJV)*

MORNING PRAYERS

God,

I want to say thanks for being with me each day, from the moment I open my eyes to when I abide in Your rest. Please show me the errors of my ways so that I can be cleansed from my sins.

God, help me to look to You always for guidance before I muddle my life. I want to continue to trust in You so that I may lead others to You. You alone are holy. I remain Your humble servant.

Amen.

Lord,

Stay with me as I navigate my daily activities. I surrender all the burdens that the world has mercilessly thrown at my feet. Lord, help me keep my gaze only on You as I stay humble. Remind me of my identity and why You marked me. Help me renew my mind and always seek You as I pursue Your purpose for me on earth. This I ask only in Your name.

Amen.

Lord,

Thank You for another glorious day. I desperately want You to stay closest to me today. Help me choose my words carefully. Anyone that I encounter, treat them the way I want to be treated, no matter how they come across. Remind me to focus on *Proverbs 15:1* (KJV): "A soft word turneth away wrath: but grievous words stir up anger. I want your spirit to channel through me today."

Lord, I always want to be aware of Your presence in my life. I surrender all to You today. I am at Your mercy, as I remember that it's Your will, not mine.

Lord, I know You will guide me through this day so that I can come out victorious. Help me focus on You only. This I ask in Your name.

Amen.

Father,

You are the mist that I feel on my face as I take my daily morning walk. You always give me the strength to keep going, although at times I may feel like giving up. When the tempest rolls, You help me navigate the waves and get me safely to the shores. My hope lies only in You.

Thank You so much for your encouragement. I am so elated that You believe in me, and I am Your special child. You deserve all the glory, Lord.

Amen.

DRAWING CLOSER TO GOD

As you draw closer to God, He will definitely draw closer to you. *Psalm 36:5* (KJV) says, "Thy mercy, O Lord, is in the heavens: and thy faithfulness reacheth unto the clouds." It reminds us of the Lord's promise. His love and mercy know no bounds. His love is so wonderful! God will give His all to save each of us. We are special to Him. His love for us is so enormous that He will force His way through any depth just to bring us closer to Him.

There is a song that I truly adore. It begins like this:

> The love of God is greater than any tongue can tell. It goes beyond the highest star, and richest the lowest hell. The wandering child is reconciled by God's beloved Son. The aching soul again made whole, and priceless pardon won.

This is just the first verse. This song was written in 1917 by Frederick M. Lehman as he was going through hardship. After losing everything he had worked for, he kept his faith. The song also says that God's love is measureless and pure. Oh yes! It is. His love never drifts away. It's abundant and unconfined. All we have to do is give credence to it.

Each time I hear or sing those lyrics, it touches the depth of my being. That song has, for me, one of the most powerful lyrics ever written. One cannot listen to this song and not believe there is a higher power than us. I urge you to obtain a copy.

Also, get acquainted with Frances Jane Van Alstyne, also known as Fanny Crosby. This wonderful woman wrote over eight thousand songs, which include "Blessed Assurance," "To God Be the Glory,"

"Jesus Is Tenderly Calling," and "Pass Me Not, O Gentle Savior." These hymns send a compelling message of faith. Fanny Cosby was named the "Queen of Gospel Songwriters."

At six weeks, she went blind, but despite being blind, she had remarkable talent. She played the piano, organ, and harp. It was said that at ten years of age, she memorized five chapters of the Bible each week. Fanny Crosby had many challenges in her lifetime, but through it all, she never abandoned God. It was said that she believed that her blindness was a gift from God, for it allowed her to focus on her writing without the distractions of the world.

Please research Fanny Crosby so that you can learn about this wonderful Christian woman.

There are times when we seek God's protection and guidance, and we become overwhelmed by what is going on in the world. It sometimes makes us lose the sense of God's presence. It shouldn't happen, but it does. Still, through all our doubts, hurt, distrust, fears, and misgivings, it is comforting to know that God is with us. Through the presence of the Holy Spirit, God is constantly and fully present.

Aren't we blessed to know that not only is He with us, but He also lives in us and is working through us? However, we must open our hearts to let Him in. We can't only call on the Lord when good things happen in our lives; we have to call on Him because He is good.

SCRIPTURES FOR JOY/PEACE

Blessed is the man that walketh not in the counsel of the ungodly, not standeth in the way of sinners, not sitteth in the seat of the scornful. But his delight is in the law of the Lord; and in his law doth meditate day and night. And he shall be like a tree planted by the river of the water, that bringeth forth his fruit in his season; his leaf also shall not wither; and whatsoever he doeth shall prosper. *(Psalm 1:1–3 KJV)*

I know that there is no good in them, but for a man to rejoice, and to do good in his life. And also that every man should eat and drink, and enjoy the good of all his labor, it is the gift of God. *(Ecclesiastes 3:12–13 KJV)*

My brethren, count it all joy when ye fall into divers temptation; knowing this, that the trying of your faith worketh patience. *(James 1:2–3 KJV)*

Let not your heart be troubled; ye believe in God, believe also in me. In my Father's house are many mansions: if it were not so, I would have told you. I go and prepare a place for you. *(John 14:1–2 KJV)*

The righteous cry out and the Lord heareth, and delivereth them out of all their troubles. The Lord is nigh unto them that are of a broken heart, and saveth such as be of a contrite spirit. Many are the affliction of the righteous, but the Lord delivereth him out of them all. He keepeth all his bones, not one of them broken. *(Psalm 34:17–20 KJV)*

And the peace of God, which passeth all understanding, shall keep your hearts and minds through Christ Jesus. *(Philippians 4:7 KJV)*

And the Lord, he it is that doth go before thee; he will be with thee, he will not fail thee, neither forsake thee: fear not, neither be dismayed. *(Deuteronomy 31:8 KJV)*

MOUNTAIN VS. VALLEY

My personal belief is that God will put us through trials just to see, as they say, if we have the right stuff to stay on the road to Calvary. I also know that, as human beings, we will fall short at times; nonetheless, it doesn't mean we cannot ask our merciful God for forgiveness. All we have to do is confess our sins to Him so that we can rejoin His fold. It states in *1 John 1:9* (KJV), "If we confess our sins, he is faithful and just to forgive us our sins, and to cleanse us from all unrighteousness."

Down in the valley is one of the hardest places to be, speaking of a rock and a harder place. There were times in my life when I was struggling, and my faith wavered. Things were very difficult for me. I knew what I had to do, but I could never get my heart right. I wrestled with my conscience as I talked to God sometimes. I was going through life as though I was the one in charge. I left God completely out of the picture. I completely forget the times when He placed me so lofty on the mountain and all the blessings that He had given me. Hence, when the bad times surfaced, they overshadowed my mountain glory. I needed clarity.

I found a way, in my dark despair. I cried out to my Lord. I came to realize that he never left me; he pulled me through. He was there all the time. I clung to Him. It's called earnest prayer. I had nothing to lose.

When all hope is gone, you get down on your knees, even reluctantly, and just surrender. Yes, there were times that I fell, but I know that the love God had for me was never broken.

When things are going well for us, it's so easy to keep the faith. Then when the storms start battering our doors, we lose hope. Hope means to trust and wait for something to happen. Therefore, without hope, we are nothing. We, as followers of God, must have a strong yearning for His goodness and grace. We have to remember that no matter what we are struggling with, the same God is always there. We just have to dig deeper and overcome.

In *Psalm 143:4–6* (KJV),

> Therefore is my spirit overwhelmed within me, my heart within me is desolate. I remember the days of old; I meditate on all thy works; I muse on the works of thy hands. I stretched forth my hands unto thee: my soul thirsteth after thee, as a thirsty land.

This is one of my favorite verses. It keeps me grounded. Let's continue our walk in faith, trusting in God's mercy and grace. We must all try harder to attain a higher knowledge and understanding of Him. Our hearts must be open.

What a mighty God we serve!

Tell me. Have you ever seen a plant blooming where it seems impossible for anything to grow? Yet it took root. Or Have you seen a bird trying to suck nectar from a dried flower? Take a look at the hardworking ants. When they lose their food, they go back and start over. One must admire their tenacity. These creatures are amazing to come across because they never give up until they have accomplished what they set out to do. Even they have hope. We should all be like God's creatures and plants—relentless.

God will never leave, especially when we are in despair. He will never desert us. Please don't ever give up, my friends. God has given us a book called the Bible. In this wonderful book, you will find the answers you are searching for. *Joshua 1:8* (KJV) states,

> This book of the law shall not depart out of my mouth, but thou shalt meditate therein day and night, that thou mayest observe to do according to all that is written therein: For thou

> shalt make thy way prosperous, and thou have good success.

What a precious word to live by!

We have to remember to pray. *Thessalonians 5:16–18* (KJV) reminds us, "Rejoice, evermore. Pray without ceasing. In everything give thanks, for this is the will of God in Christ Jesus concerning you."

He wants us to have a beneficial life.

PRAYERS FOR COMFORT

Lord,

Sometimes, I don't know where to turn, but knowing that You are always there, navigating my direction, eases my burden. I am so grateful that You are with me every step of the way. I know, Lord, that You will never leave me. For this, I am indebted.

Amen.

God,

I have no doubt that You love me. I always want to stay with You so that You can be my sanctuary. When things in this world become too much and I can't lift my head above the noise and confusion, help me to look up for Your extended hand.

I know that all my emotions are under Your control when I place them within You.

Lord, I ask for comfort and healing in times of need.

This I ask only in Your name.

Amen.

Lord,

Sometimes, my heart breaks, and I feel all choked up and sometimes confused. I can't find the right words to communicate. Sometimes my self-assurance is broken. I need You, Lord, to work through all my dejections with me.

Lord, I pray that You will heal my lacerations. Help me accept setbacks without so much discomfort.

This I ask, in Your name only.

Amen.

Lord,

You are my refuge and my strength. When You walk with me in my daily life, I confide in You as I tell You all my heartaches. As I lay down to rest, You quieted my pounding heart.

Lord, all I ask is calmness. Slow me down, and please allow me to keep pace with You.

Everything that I am is because of You. All my hope starts with You!

Amen.

God,

Sometimes I am overwhelmed with the loss I feel. Although my heart is broken, I know that I am covered by Your grace and love. These times are the times that I place all my cares in your hand because I know that, in my darkest hour of need, you embrace me and give me strength.

I pray that one day when all my sufferings are over, you will shower me with Your love, especially when we unite in glory.

Amen.

SCRIPTURES FOR COMFORT

Wait on the Lord: be of good courage, and he shall strengthen thine heart: wait, I say, on the Lord. *(Psalm 27:14 KJV)*

Come unto me, all ye that labour and are heavy laden, and I will give you rest. *(Matthew 11:28 KJV)*

Blessed be God, even the Father of our Lord Jesus Christ, the Father of mercies, and the God of all comfort. Who comfort us in all our tribulation, that we may be able to comfort them which are in any trouble, by the comfort wherewith we ourselves are comforted of God. *(2 Corinthians 1:3–4 KJV)*

Behold, I am, the Lord, the God of all flesh: is there anything too hard for me? *(Jeremiah 32:27 KJV)*

Casting all your care upon him; for he careth for you? *(1 Peter 5:7 KJV)*

Fear not, little flock; for it is your Father's good pleasure to give you the kingdom. *(Luke 12:32 KJV)*

For God so loved the world, that he gave his only begotten Son, that whosoever believeth in him should not perish, but have everlasting life. *(John 3:16 KJV)*

JESUS LOVES THE LITTLE CHILDREN

Children are cherished gifts from God, as *Psalm 127:3* (KJV) states, "Lo children are an heritage of the Lord, and the fruit of the womb is the reward." How precious are these words? The song "Jesus loves the little children, all the children in the world," written by Clarence Herbert Woolston and tuned by George Frederick Root, is beautiful and inspiring. It tells how precious they are to God.

As Christian adults, we have to teach the children how to walk in the Lord while still young so they know what God has planned for them if they stay true to His Word. As Christians, we must shepherd our children to become disciples of Jesus. We also want them to have a durable relationship with the Bible. We must remind them that God is all around, and His love for us never fluctuates, like humans. David reminds us in *Psalm 136* (KJV), "For his mercy endureth forever."

The most important legacy that one can leave their children is the wisdom of God's love. *Deuteronomy 6:7* (KJV) states, "And thou shalt teach them diligently unto thy children, and shalt talk of them when thou sittest in thine house, and when thou walkest by the way, and when thou liest down, and when thou risest up." He wants all knowledge about Him to be passed from generation to generation.

We must raise God-fearing children. They have to be exposed to a Christian community. Take them to church every time while encouraging them to serve in the church during the mass. We cannot wait until they are in their teenage years before bringing them to God. We must lead by example. These young, impressionable minds mimic everything we do.

Treat our children the way you want to be treated, so that when they are around their peers, it will be a reflection of us.

Raising a child is very hard work, especially if you are a single parent. I can attest to that, so we must show the same grace that our Lord and Savior shows us. As Christians, we must know how to speak with our children. In Colossians 4:6 (KJV), we are reminded, "Let you, speech be always with grace, season with salt, that ye may know how ye ought to answer every man."

This world is a very scary place for our children. Too many unpleasant things are happening. In my youth, growing up in the West Indies, I can say things were a lot simpler. My family had no television, no Internet services, and no Facebook, WhatsApp, or TikTok. We were sheltered from the dangers that lurked. Most of our time was spent reading books that were designed to enhance our lives. For any information that we needed for school, we had to look it up in an encyclopedia or rely on our teacher's knowledge. Most things were designed to keep our minds clear and to shelter us from the outside world. Still, things happened, but not like what I hear today.

I must admit that change is good. It is important for us to enhance our lives. It's called progress. My worry is that the Internet exposes children to so much bad content, and if we are not conscientious and diligent, they can fall prey to some unscrupulous individuals.

Then we have those unsupervised children who are left on their own. I do understand that parents are so busy juggling so many tasks, especially single parents.

Children will text with people they don't know and play video games designed to mess up their young minds. All these things are detrimental to our youth, so as adults and Christians, we must make sure that they are always supervised. I wonder, with all the advancement in technology that's floating around, is it doing more harm than good to our precious little ones? Our little ones need direction and lots of motivation.

We have to give them the wisdom and courage to make the best choice. Children must grow up with a strong sense of purpose and belonging.

Let's move them forward on a godly path. Steer them from walking so carelessly into evil. For this is our job as good Christians. In *Ephesians 5:15–17* (KJV), it states, "See then that we walk circumspectly, not as fools, but as wise. Redeeming the time, because the days are evil. Wherefore be ye not unwise, but understanding what the will of the Lord is."

Let us, as adults and Christians, take the lead.

Anytime a child is treated badly, it pains God. It is written in *Matthew 18:10* (KJV), "Take heed that ye despise not one of these little ones: for I say unto you, that in heaven their angels do always behold the face of my Father which is in heaven."

Let's teach all the children to pray now. They will not do it if not taught. Equip them to be messengers for Christ.

Remember, Jesus loves us all without condition.

SCRIPTURES FOR CHILDREN

Whosoever shall receive one of such children in my name, receiveth me: and whosoever shall receive me, receiveth not me, but he that sent me. *(Mark 9:37 KJV)*

And all thy children shall be taught of the LORD; and great shall be the peace of thy children. In righteousness shalt thou be established: thou shall be far from oppression; for thou shalt not fear: and from terror; for it shall not come near thee. *(Isaiah 54:13 KJV)*

I have no greater joy than to hear that my children walketh in the truth. *(3 John 1:4 KJV)*

A woman when she is in travail hath sorrow, because her hour is come, but as soon as she delivered of the child, she remembered no more the anguish, for the joy that a child is born in the world. *(John 16:21 KJV)*

Lo, children are an heritage of the Lord: and the fruit of the womb is his reward. As arrows are in the hand of a mighty man; so are the children of thy youth. Happy is the man that hath his quiver full of them; they shall not be ashamed, but they shall speak with the enemies in the gate. *(Psalm 127:3–5 KJV)*

PRAYERS FOR THE CHILDREN

Lord,

As my children take their journey out into the world, I give them all to You. I am placing them ever so gently in your loving arms so that I may release my worries and have peace—perfect peace.

I know that You will protect them as they go about their busy day. Lord, remind them to also give You thanks and prayers for staying so closely by their side. Help them not to feel anxious, no matter what situation they may encounter. I ask You, Lord, to bring them back safely home when the day has ended.

This I ask in Your name.

Amen.

God,

Thank You for all the precious little ones. Thank You for instilling in our hearts Your word and love so that we can pass it on to them. Help us to give them guidance, and thank You for keeping them protected.

Lord, for all the other children in the world, I also ask for Your protection. Wrap Your loving arm around them, especially those who are facing war or famine. Give us a soft heart to help us share what we have with them, even if it is small.

I know that I can rest just knowing that they are loved by You. This I ask in Your name.

Amen.

Lord,

Thank You for my child/children, whom you have placed in my care until the day that they return to You. Help them to show mercy and grace to others as You have shown me.

I want You to direct me on how to teach them love and respect for You daily because You alone are holy, Lord. The scripture *1 Samuel 12:24* (KJV) says, "Only fear the Lord and serve him in truth with all your heart: for consider how great things he hath done for you."

Lord, I want to honor Your words as I continue to instill Your love for them. I want them to love and know You so much that nothing in this world will deter them from You.

This I ask in Your name.

Amen.

Lord,

As my child/children venture out today, I ask for Your protection over them. For I know that once they go through that door and I can no longer see them, You have guardianship over them. I will give them all to You.

Help them to show respect for me, their friends, teachers, and others who they may encounter along the way. Lord, help them to choose their words carefully and to show no disdain toward others.

Please guide them to make the correct decision and steer them away from any danger.

Help them when making friendly bonds to use discernment while guiding others to You.

This I ask in Your name only.

Amen.

Father,

I am grateful. Thank You for such wonderful gifts—our children. I ask that You keep them healthy and safe and surround them with happiness.

Lord, I pray for the children who are suffering, especially those who suffer from illness, poverty, abuse, or neglect. I ask for Your blessings, as the adults give them strength and support to rise above their challenges.

For those who are suffering from mental health issues, comfort them and help them and their families find the resources that are needed to heal them. I ask that they be embraced with love, lots of support, and great role models, for they need to thrive and grow with a sense of purpose.

Continue blessing all the children so that the world will not be such a scary place but a place where they can reach their full potential and bloom.

In Your name,

Amen.

GROWING OLD GRACEFULLY IN GOD'S PRESENCE

It may be hard for some to come to terms with the idea of growing old. They are reminded daily, from the moment they awake, of the things they can no longer do. One must remember that it's a natural process, and the longer we live, the sooner it is bound to happen. It's a consequence that is quite inevitable; besides, getting older is a blessing.

Keep in mind that as we age, we are growing wiser. *Job 12:12* (KJV) says, "Is not wisdom found among the aged? Does not long life bring understanding?" In the Bible, it says that God will be with us. He will never turn His back on us. He reminds us that He will stay with us, especially when we are tired. As it says in *Psalm 73:26* (KJV): "My flesh and my heart faileth: but God is the strength of my heart, and my portion forever." These are wonderful words to keep in our minds.

Growing old gracefully with God is a journey where we must have a lot of commitment. It is a process of spiritual growth in which we show maturity, and it allows us to continue to live meaningful and fulfilling lives. When we grasp a deeper comprehension of His love and His plans for our lives, then we will know what purpose we have to fulfill in this life.

As Christians, a personal relationship with God is a requirement. As we read the Bible, we must pause at times and reflect on each word. We must lean on Him for guidance and listen to His commands. We must remember that we are on God's journey, and it requires dedication, tenacity, and preparedness to learn and grow.

The Lord our God has given us so many blessings, even through all our struggles. These are things that we should appreciate, as He prepares in us a spirit of gratitude. So when we stay in Christ, we will realize that He is training our hearts and minds to develop a positive attitude toward Him, so we have to be deeply committed, walking as Christ would have us walk. We must walk circumspectly by living wisely, morally, and carefully. We, as Christians, must be obedient to every commandment that God has handed down. As we grow older, so much has changed in our outward appearances. Our body sags, and everything seems to go south, and yes, sometimes we don't like how we look, but it's not our call.

There are things that we do use to have a better youthful appearance, but I am not an advocate of going under the knife to reverse our bodies; for me, it goes much too far. I am God's temple, and I am reminded in *1 Corinthians 3:16–17* (KJV):

> Know ye not that ye are the temple of God, and that the Spirit of God dwelleth in you? If any man defiles the temple of God, him shall God destroy; for the temple of God is holy, which temple ye are.

As we grow older, our faith is on full display. Let us all embrace our mustard seed moment. Let's all aspire to move mountains. Also, don't let the enemy distract our hope, for it's our magnet. The Lord God manifests in your life, so don't do it alone. As we grow older, we acquire more wisdom; we have so much to teach the youth. We have to open our minds to new perspectives and be willing to release old habits that can only hinder us from moving forward. Just try to be the wonderful person that God made you to be.

To conclude, we must keep in mind that we are on God's journey, and this requires dedication and an open mind to learn and grow. Serving others is a good first step.

There, our purpose may become known. Remember what Paul said in Philippians *1:6 (KJV)*, “Being confident of this very thing, that which hath begun a good work in you will perform it until the day of Jesus Christ.”

PRAYERS FOR GROWING OLDER

Lord,

Please always remind me that I am never alone. I ask for courage as I start my day and to always have a positive outlook.

As the day continues, remind me that my body and mind are not as quick as they were when I was much younger. Please give me the patience to accept that reality. Lord, when I am offered help, let me accept it gracefully and not let my pride get in the way.

As I get older, I ask that my mind stay sharp. I just want to retain a sense of purpose and maintain my independence. I ask for your love and guidance as I cruise around this new era of my life. I ask that You keep me grateful and humble. This I ask in Your name.

Amen.

> For which cause we faint not; but though our outward man perish, yet the inward man is renewed day by day. For our light afflictions, which is but for a moment, worketh for us a far more exceeding and eternal weight of glory; while we look not at the things which are seen, but the things which are not seen: for the things which are seen are temporal; but the things which are not seen are eternal. *(2 Corinthians 4:16–18* KJV*)*

Father,

I am indebted to You for the gift of my parent(s). Thank You for all the sacrifices that they have made throughout the years. I ask for continuous blessings for good health and renewed strength as their days lessen.

Lord, I also ask for comfort and quiet as their days progress, along with much joy and happiness. Surround them with Your precious love as I leave them in Your hands because I know You will protect them as they navigate these new chapters of their lives.

I ask in your holy name.

Amen.

Lord,

Today, especially, I am extending my prayers, asking for Your healing touch on my mind and body. For I know that You are the greatest physician, so I place all my care and trust in Your loving hands.

I am asking for health for my physical body as my days dwindle. I need restoration to increase my knowledge of You. Lord, soothe my emotional wounds, my anxiety, and my fears. I just need a tiny bit of comfort at times.

I am placing all that I am in Your loving hands. I give You all the glory for all the blessings that I have already received.

I ask for Your continued guidance as I stay on the narrow road to You.

I pray for all this in Your name.

Amen.

God,

I bow down to You, asking for Your healing hands on my loved ones, others, and myself, who suffer daily. I know that You are the reliever of all pain, and nothing is impossible for You.

I am asking that You shower me with Your healing powers. I also ask for strength and courage to handle what's ahead of me in life and to do so in peace and comfort, for this world is fueled by pain and uncertainty.

Instill a level of compassion in all the doctors and nurses if I ever have to be cared for by them by allowing them to be guided by You as they administer their healing touch. I know that You are with me every step of my life's journey. I ask this prayer in faith, for I know that You can do immeasurably more than I can ever imagine.

In Your name only.

Amen.

SCRIPTURES FOR THE ELDERLY

But if any provide no for his own, and specially for those of his own house, he hath denied faith, and is worse than an infidel. *(1 Timothy 5:8 KJV)*

Remember the days of old. Consider the years of many generations; ask thy father, and he will shew thee; thy elders, and they will tell thee. *(Deuteronomy 32:7 KJV)*

Say not thou, What is the cause that the former days were better than these? For thou doesn't enquire wisely concerning this. *(Ecclesiastes 7:10 KJV)*

With the ancient is wisdom, and in the length of days understanding. *(Job 12:12 KJV)*

For which cause we faint; but though our outward man perishes, yet the inward man is renewed day by day. For our light afflictions, which is but for a moment worketh for us a far more exceeding and eternal weight of glory. While we look not at the things which are seen, but at the things which are not seen; for the things which are seen are temporal; but the things which are not seen are eternal. *(2 Corinthians 4:16–18 KJV)*

But they that wait on the Lord shall renew their strength; they shall mount up with wings as eagles; they shall run, and not be weary; and they shall walk and not faint. *(Isaiah 40:31 KJV)*

PRAYERS OF AN ANONYMOUS ABBESS

Lord,

Thou knowest better than myself, that I am growing older and soon would be old. Keep me from becoming too talkative, and especially from the unfortunate habit of thinking that I must say something on every subject, and at every opportunity.

Release me from the idea that I must straighten out other people's affairs. With my immense treasure of experience and wisdom, it seems a pity not to let everybody partake of it. But thou knowest, Lord, that in the end I will need a few friends.

Keep me from the recital of endless detail; give me wings to get to the point.

Grant me the patience to listen to the complaints of others; help me to endure them with charity. But seal my lips on my own aches and pains-they increase with the increasing years, and my inclination to recount them is also increasing.

I will not ask thee for improved memory. Only for a little more humility and less self-assurance when my own memory doesn't agree with that of others.

Teach me the glorious lesson that occasionally I may be wrong.

Amen.

POEMS FOR GROWING OLDER

1
As I soldier on life's journey
I feel my youth and strength decrease.
Then as I try not to think about it,
I am reminded when they both pervade.

The days go by. Yes! They slip away.
My gray hair shows, my joint makes noise.
My hearing and sight keep pace too. All I do now is feel my years.
Lord! It's real. I need more grace.

As I cling to what is dear to me
My wisdom deepens, lines on my face stare back.
That's when the memories become so clear.
But my hope for You will never fade.

I am thankful, hopelessness doesn't invade me.
For deep in my heart, I have a youthful zest.
My life now is no longer about autumn.
It's more like when the sun begins to set.

As I prepare to meet my Savior,
I know I have lived and conquered fear.
For in my heart, I am reminded,
There, I will find my deepest truth.

2

When I see the lines on my face
I know it's about memories I won't erase.
And as I watch my hair turn gray.
My spirit glints through all day

I have increased my knowledge through the years.
Now I know much more of God's love, wisdom, and grace.
I will accept this aging life
And walk into it with much delight.

So as my body now grows weaker.
Guess what? My spirit stays young and grows much bolder
Then as the days pass by my way
I will find new joy to call my own.

I will age with grace and poise.
When I raise my head, with each new morn.
My body grows tired, but the spirit in me
Will never die through eternity.

JESUS LOVES ME (SENIOR STYLE)

Jesus loves me this I know
Though my hair is white as snow
Though my sight is growing dim
Still He bids me trust in Him

Chorus:
Yes, Jesus loves me. Yes, Jesus loves me
Yes, Jesus loves me. The Bible tells me so

Though my steps are oh-so-slow
With my hand in His lap, I'll go
On through life, let come my way
He will be there to lead the way

Chorus:
Yes, Jesus loves me. Yes, Jesus loves me
Yes, Jesus loves me. The Bible tells me so

Though I am no longer young
I have much which He's begun
Let me serve Christ with a smile!
Go with others the extra mile.

Chorus:
Yes, Jesus loves me. Yes, Jesus me
Yes, Jesus loves me. The Bible tells me so.

When the height is dark and long
In my heart, He puts a song
Telling me in words so clear
Have no fear, for I am near!

Chorus:
Yes, Jesus loves me. Yes, Jesus loves me
Yes, Jesus loves me. The Bible tells me so

When my work on earth is done.
And life's victories have been won
He will take me home above
Then I'll understand His love.

Yes, Jesus loves me. Yes, Jesus loves me.
Yes, Jesus loves me. The Bible tells me so.

(Anon)

PRAYERS FOR HUMILITY

Grant me, Lord, to always have someone around to watch me as I grow older. Lord, when I want more things in my life, please allow me to see that I already have plenty. Remind me that some don't have as much as I do, so I should always be grateful.

Help me to treat others the way I want to be treated and to be sympathetic to their feelings.

Lord, before I respond to anything that was said in a negative way to me, remind me to always count to ten so that my thoughts will be mixed with salt and my words can be seasoned before I ever open my mouth. Remind me that I am not in control of others' thoughts and behaviors. I am just what You see in me, Lord.

Draw me closer to those who have considered me an enemy because of a miscommunication. One more thing, Lord. I want to continue growing in Your wisdom while strengthening my walk with You. I am asking that You allow a humble seed to foster within me. Amen.

Father,

I want to say thanks for being with me every day from the moment I opened my eyes. Please show me the errors of my way so that I may be cleansed from my sins. Help me to look to You always for guidance in all that I do before I walk in my own way.

I want to continue to place my trust in You so that my faith may bring others to You because You alone are holy, Lord.

I remain Your respectful servant, Lord.

Amen.

Lord,

Stay with me as I work through my day. I will lay down all the burdens that the world has thrown at my feet. I cannot carry them alone. Help me to stay humble as my eyes stay fixed on You.

Amen.

SCRIPTURES FOR HUMILITY

By humility and the fear of the Lord are riches, and honor and life. *(Proverbs 22:4 KJV)*

Humble yourselves in the sight of the Lord, and he shall lift you up. *(James 4:10 KJV)*

He hath shewed thee, O man, what is good; and what doth the Lord require of thee, but to do so justly, and to love mercy, and to walk humbly with thy God? *(Micah 6:8 KJV)*

Let nothing be done through strife or vainglory; but in lowliness of mind let each esteem others better than ourselves. *(Philippians 2:3 KJV)*

Likewise, ye younger, submit yourselves unto the elder. Yea, all of you be subject one to another, and be clothed with humility: for God resisteth the proud, and giveth grace to the humble. *(1 Peter 5:5 KJV)*

Surely he scorneth the scorners: but he giveth grace unto the lowly. *(Proverbs 3:34 KJV)*

PRAYERS OF GRATITUDE

Lord,

Thanks for being with me as You shoulder my every load. When the road gets too rough for me, I am glad I have You to lean on. You alone are my strength and my hiding place. Unto You, I cling. Lord, help me not to take advice that is not well intended.

I will always look to You first.

Amen.

Father,

Where You have planted me, help me to embrace it with all my heart. Enhance my vision so that I can see all the wonderful things that You have placed right in front of me. Remind me that I am Your child and that I am extra special.

Father, help me to develop the gift of discernment so that all my thoughts will be clear. Thanks for the grace and mercy You have bestowed on me. Let my thoughts and prayers always be focused on You. This I ask in Your name.

Amen.

Lord,

You alone are my sustainer. There are times when I worry about what this world renders. Then, Lord, I realize that relationships, the best clothes, and lots of money are all fleeting.

Lord, I can put my head comfortably at night on my pillow in deep satisfaction, knowing You are all I need. Help me to always remember this.

Amen.

SCRIPTURES FOR GRATITUDE

But thanks be to God, which giveth us the victory through our Lord Jesus Christ. *(1 Corinthians 15:57 KJV)*

I will praise thee. O Lord, with my whole heart, I will shew forth all thy marvelous works. *(Psalm 9:1 KJV)*

And he took bread, and gave thanks, and broke it, and gave unto them, saying This is my body which I have given for you: this do in remembrance of me. *(Luke 22:19 KJV)*

For every creature of God Is good, and nothing to be refused, if it be received with thanksgiving. *(1 Timothy 4:4 KJV)*

In everything give thanks; for this is the will of God in Christ Jesus concerning you. *(1 Thessalonians 5:18 KJV)*

Saying, We give thanks O Lord God Almighty, which art and wast, and art to come; because thou hast taken to thee they great power, and hast reigned. (*Revelations 11:17 KJV*)

PRAYERS IN TROUBLED TIMES

Lord,

The last few months have been a challenge. If it wasn't for You, I would have fallen on my face. There are times when problems take over, and I can't see the victorious life You have in store for me. But when those times surface, I am reminded of what is written in *John 16:33* (KJV): "These things I have spoken unto you, that in ye might have peace. In the world ye shall have tribulation: but be of good cheer; I have overcome the world."

Thank You for those words, Lord. They keep me grounded and remind me to never look away from You no matter the circumstance so that my heart can receive Your love.

Amen.

Lord,

We are all sinners. We know what we must do, but sometimes we fall short of what You expect from us. Our human side takes over, and evil is always waiting to send us spiraling out in the other direction. Lord, allow us to keep the faith, as the Bible says what we should do about staying in Your good grace. The scripture *2 Peter 3:18* reminds us, "But grow in grace, and in the knowledge of our Lord and Savior Jesus Christ. To him be glory both now and forever."

Help us to hold on to Your will while holding steadfast to our faith as we keep You at the forefront of our hearts and minds.

Amen.

Father,

Sometimes, I feel like a hamster, just running around on an endless wheel. It is hard to navigate every twist and turn of my life. Thank You for showing me mercy so that I can keep my head above the water that sometimes wants to engulf my soul.

Remind me always that I am made in Your likeness and that You love me so much You sent Your beloved son to die for me. Help me walk circumspectly always as I stay true to You.

Lord, wrap Your loving arms around me as You keep me safe from all the wicked intentions of others. Give me discernment to always listen as You speak.

Lord, keep me away from any negative influences or any distractions that may knock me off balance, and, Lord, You know there are many.

I ask that You keep my heart pure and my mind alert as I grow older, embracing the life that You envisioned for me.

I humbly ask these things in Your name.

Amen.

SCRIPTURES FOR TROUBLED TIMES

Now the God of hope fills you with all joy and peace in believing that ye may abound in hope, through the power of the Holy Ghost. *(Romans 15:13 KJV)*

Thou wilt keep him in perfect peace, whose mind is stayed on thee; because he trusteth in thee. (*Isaiah 26:3 KJV)*

Commit thy way unto the Lord, trust also in him; and he shall bring it to pass. *(Psalm 37:5 KJV)*

When thou passest through the waters, I will be with thee; and through the rivers, they shall not overflow thee: when thou walkest through the fire, thou shalt not be burned, neither shall they flames kindle upon thee. *(Isaiah 43:2 KJV)*

Behold, I am the Lord, the God of all flesh: is there anything too hard for me? *(Jeremiah 32:27 KJV)*

Knowing this, that the trying of your faith worketh patience. *(James 1:3 KJV)*

The name of the Lord is a strong tower: the righteous runneth into it, and is safe. *(Proverbs 18:10 KJV)*

PRAYERS FOR STRENGTH

Lord,

At times, life takes a toll on me. I am left tossing and turning before I find a comfortable place to rest. The pain that I feel every so often is more than I can bear. It zaps my strength, but I place all my trust and hope in You.

As I get older, I don't want to feel any contrition about anything that I have done. *Isaiah 43:18–19* (KJV) states, "Forget the former things; don't dwell on the past. I am clinging to those trusting words."

I have to also remember that Christ already saved me by His blood, and there is no condemnation in Christ Jesus.

Keep my eyes and heart on the rewards that You have already stored up for me. Help me to run and never grow weary and walk and not faint, as *Isaiah 40:31* reminds me.

I want to keep my hope in You, Lord.

Amen.

Lord,

I am asking for You to strengthen my life. Because You are my only refuge, and I am convinced that You are beside me in my troubled times.

Psalm 28:7 (KJV) says, "The Lord is my strength and my shield: my heart trusts in him, and I am helped; Therefore my heart greatly rejoiceth; and with my song will I praise him."

I am so comforted each time I feel Your presence. Because in You, I find peace, and my strength is renewed.

I know You walk with me as You steady my feeble footsteps. I am asking day by day to strengthen them, for I know You will be my guide, and You are all the courage that I will ever need.

This I ask in Your name.

Amen.

God,

I am asking that You go before me today so that no matter what I face today, my heart will be filled with joy.

My mind will be open, enjoying all the goodness You have already bestowed on me. Lord, I ask for strength to continue my journey to You. Turn any despair I have into hope. Help me to walk boldly into the future without feeling fear. I ask in Your name only.

Amen.

SCRIPTURES FOR STRENGTH

He giveth power to the faint; and to them that have no might he increaseth strength. *(Isaiah 40:29 KJV)*

Seek the Lord and his strength, seek his face continually. *(1 Chronicles 16:11 KJV)*

Finally, my brethren, be strong in the Lord, and in the power of his might. (*Ephesians 6:10* KJV)

My flesh and my heart faileth: but God is the strength of my heart, and my portion forever. *(Psalm 73:26 KJV)*

And let us not weary in well doing: for in due season we shall reap. If we faint not. *(Galatians 6:9 KJV)*

And not only so, be we glory in tribulations also; knowing that tribulations worketh patience. And patience, experience, and experience hope. *(Romans 5:3–4 KJV)*

Behold, God is my salvation, I will trust, and not be afraid, for the Lord Jehovah is my strength and my song, he also is my salvation. *(Isaiah 12:2 KJV)*

For the Lord your God is he that goeth with you, to fight for you against your enemies, to save you. (*Deuteronomy 20:4* KJV)

PRAYERS FOR COMFORT

Father,

Thank You for staying with me. At times, it feels as though I am always at a crossroads, but I know that although the journey is sometimes strenuous, as Your child, I am never alone.

The dawn is the darkest and hardest place to encounter. Nevertheless, I always feel your presence as you steer me out of the valley while I carry all my burdens. With You always in front, beside, above, and behind me, it becomes more bearable.

It is written in *John 14:18* (KJV), "I will never leave you comfortless. I will come to you." Thank You from the depths of my heart. For this, I will always remain Your faithful servant. How wonderful to abide in Your love!

Amen.

Lord,

It's written in *Psalm 118:24* (KJV), "This is the day that the Lord has made, we will rejoice and be glad in it." As I face a brand-new day, this verse resonates within me. As I look out over the rooftops of the buildings that I see before me, Your wonderful creation, the sun casts a glow across my face. I humbly give You thanks. I thank You for loving me, a sinner. I will submit everything to You on this day.

Remind me to always be faithful to you as my steps become less hurried, and my days dwindle. Teach me, O Lord, to never claim anything in this world as mine.

I have no idea what Your plans are for me for the rest of my life, but I know You are way ahead of me.

May I always be a helper to someone, even if it's in the smallest way. I ask for wisdom, too, as my day progresses.

Amen.

Lord,

As I grow older, I know that whatever happens, it could be much worse. I always try to see the beauty in any outcome. No matter what I am dealt with, Lord, I am thankful that I am still here. I place all my hope in You, Lord, because it's written in Your words. Lord, You are my Savior, my redeemer, and my only refuge. I am so elated that nothing in this world is difficult for You because You control all things.

Amen.

SCRIPTURES FOR COMFORT

Blessed are the peacemakers: for they shall be called the children of God. *(Matthew 5:9 KJV)*

Casting all your care upon him; for he careth for you. *(1 Peter 5:7 KJV)*

For God is not the author of confusion; but peace, as in all churches of the saints. *(1 Corinthians 14:33 KJV)*

Now we exhort you, brethren, warn them that are unruly, comfort the feeble minded, support the weak, be patient towards all men. *(1 Thessalonians 5:14 KJV)*

And ye now therefore have sorrow: but I will see you again, and your heart shall rejoice, and your joy no man taketh from you. *(John 16:22 KJV)*

It is of the Lord's mercies that we are not consumed, because his compassions fail not. They are new every morning: great is thy faithfulness. *(Lamentations 3:22–23 KJV)*

Thou will keep him in perfect peace, whose mind is stayed on thee, because he trusteth in thee. *(Isaiah 26:3 KJV)*

And let the peace of God rule in your hearts, to the which also ye are called in one body; and be ye thankful. Let the word of Christ dwell in you richly in all wisdom, teaching and admonishing one another in psalms and hymns and spiritual songs, singing with grace in your hearts to the Lord. And whatsoever ye do in word or deed, do all in the name of the Lord Jesus, giving thanks to God the Father by Him. *(Colossians 3:15–17 KJV)*

PRAYERS FOR HOPE

Father,

As a new day approaches, You breathe hope into my life. Each moment that You blessed me with reminds me of Your grace. Let me not take any of it lightly.

When hope seems to elude me, Your voice in my ear reminds me of Your precious love in a tender manner. There is no end to Your love, Lord.

You are always there to pick me up before I trip or hit rock bottom. All I have to do is call Your name.

Amen.

Lord,

You didn't say our path would always be smooth, but You also reminded us that You are the comforter. I rely on Your promises, Lord. Allow me to always be still as You work within me to overcome any challenge in my life.

You are my peace, Lord. I come before You on my knees, crying out for Your help. Give me strength, for I cannot carry this burden alone. I am placing all my hope and trust in You, Lord.

Let me not yield to my own understanding but to count on You.

Allow me to stay faithful, even in difficult times. I want to always soar like an eagle, run and not faint, and fly and not get weary.

In Your holy name.

Amen.

Lord,

I need hope. At times, life is so unpredictable. I get so discouraged, and when those times come, it overwhelms me. But, Lord, I know You are my hope, and the strength You display in me is remarkable. I know that Your love for me is unfailing. Help me to concentrate on Your light, as it is written in *Matthew 5:14* (KJV): "Ye are the light of the world. A city that is set on an hill cannot be hid."

Lord, for anyone who struggles with hopelessness, comfort them, so Your love will transcend through them also. We all must keep hoping and know that You will never leave us.

Amen.

SCRIPTURES FOR HOPE (KJV)

Now the God of hope fills you with all joy and peace in believing that ye may abound in hope, through the power of the Holy Ghost. *(Romans 15:13)*

And now, Lord, what wait I for? My hope is in thee. *(Psalm 39:7)*

Be strong and of good courage, fear not, nor be afraid of them: for the Lord thy God, he is that doth go with thee; he will not fail thee, nor forsake thee. *(Deuteronomy 31:6)*

But if we hope for what that we see not, then do we with patience wait for it. *(Romans 8:25)*

Blessed is the man that trusteth in the Lord, and whose the Lord is. For he shall be like a tree planted by the waters, and that spreadeth out her roots by the river, and shall not see when heat cometh, but her leaf shall be green; and shall not be careful in the year of drought, neither shall cease from yielding fruit. *(Jeremiah 17:7–8)*

The Lord is my portion, saith my soul therefore will I hope in him. (*Lamentations 3:24)*

PRAYERS FOR ANXIETY

Hear my cry, O God; attend unto my prayers. From the end of the earth will I cry unto thee, when my heart is overwhelmed: lead me to the rock that is higher than I. For thou hast been a shelter for me, and a strong tower from the enemy.

—*Psalm 61:1–3* KJV

Lord,

I want to be overflowing with Your never-ending light each and every day of my life. Bless me with hope for love and determination for strength. Remind me that everything I do is according to Your plan.

Lord, allow me to take a quiet stroll in Your marvelous illumination. Take the thorns away, so that I can have clarity as I follow You in faith!

Amen.

God,

You are above all that we do. Keep my eyes, heart, and mind always centered on You. I want to continue standing in Your presence and acknowledge all the blessings that I have. Help me to slow down from my busy days, which caused anxiety. I want You to remind me that You are the one Who gives me strength. I need Your precious peace, Lord.

Amen.

God,

When fear overtakes me, raise me and allow me to see Your truth. When the feelings hold me hostage and my breathing becomes labored, remind me to take one step at a time while You guide me.

When my emotions choke me up and I ask for calm in my soul, You whisper so gently in my ear, soothing all my thoughts.

I surrender all that I am to You, moment by moment, for I know Your love, forgiveness, and grace have set me free.

Amen.

> Because thou hast been my helper, therefore in the shadow of thy wings will I rejoice.
>
> My soul followeth hard after thee: thy right hand upholdeth me.
>
> But those that see my soul, to destroy it, shall go into the lower parts of the earth. (*Psalm 63:7–9* KJV)

SCRIPTURES FOR ANXIETY (KJV)

For the Lord thy God will hold thy right hand, saying unto thee, Fear not: I will help thee. *(Isaiah 41:13)*

Take therefore no thought of the marrow: for the morrow shall take thought for things of itself. Sufficient unto the day is the evil thereof. *(Matthew 6:34)*

Casting all your care upon him; for he careth for you. *(1 Peter 5:7)*

Heaviness in the heart of maketh it stoop: but a good word maketh it glad. *(Proverbs 12:25)*

Peace I leave with you, my peace I give unto you: not as the world giveth, give I unto you. Let not you be troubled, neither let it be afraid. *(John 14:27)*

And I will pray the Father, and he shall give you another Comforter, that he may abide with you forever; Even the Spirit of truth; whom the world cannot receive, because it seeth him not, neither knoweth him: but ye know him; for he dwelleth with you, and shall be in you. I will not leave you comfortless: I will come to you. *(John 14:16–18)*

The Lord is thy keeper: the Lord is thy shade upon thy right hand. The sun shall not smite thee by day, nor the moon by night. The Lord Shall preserve thee from all evil: he shall preserve thy soul. The Lord shall preserve thy going out and thy coming in from this time forth, and even for evermore. *(Psalm 121:5–8)*

There is therefore no condemnation to them which are in Christ Jesus, who walk not after the flesh, but after the Spirit. *(Romans 8:1)*

Every word of God is pure: he is a shield unto them that put their trust in him. *(Proverbs 30:5)*

And let the peace of God rule in your hearts, to which also ye are called in one body; and be ye thankful. *(Colossians 3:15)*

PRAYER OF THANKS

Father,

I give You all my thanks and prayers. When things are not going well with me, all I must do is call on Your holy name, and then I feel your tranquility. Just knowing You are shadowing me with Your presence allows any anxiety to dissipate because You have sovereignty over everything.

I am filled with Your joy, just thinking about what You have in store for me next. Help me, Lord, to continue growing in Your likeness, showing love and mercy to others.

This I ask in Your name.

Amen.

PRAYERS FOR LIFE

God,

I thank You for giving me the priceless gift of life. My heart's desire is to enjoy every moment of it while I use my days wisely.

I want to live a life that will always honor and glorify Your name.

Lord, please help me to make sound decisions as I decipher what is right or wrong. I want to shine my light in this conflicted world so I can talk about Your love and grace.

When difficult times interrupt my days, please allow me strength and courage to conquer them, while You walk along with me.

Lord, I know Your plans for me are good, even when they don't make sense to me. I want to always be thankful for the blessings You give me. Remind me to show kindness and compassion to all who cross my path and to be a strong carrier of Your hope. Again, Lord, thank You for my life. I want my existence to be a testimony to Your love, grace, and tender mercy.

Amen.

AFTER THE HURT

The pain and difficulty you must process when you are going through a hard time are overwhelming. Especially when emotions get the better of you. I am just adding a few prayers that helped me, as I gained a sense of peace during those times as I healed.

A PRAYER FOR WISDOM

Dear God,

I come before You, asking You to guide me through this difficult chapter in my life. I ask that You keep my mind clear as the challenges engulf me. I pray that You grant me the courage to forge ahead and rise above any obstacle.

I trust in You and all the plans that You have for me going forward.

Lord, I know You have a much bigger goal for my future.

Amen.

A PRAYER FOR HEALING

God,

I need Your help now. I am brokenhearted. Embrace me with all Your loving comfort. I am leaning on You for strength. Please clear my thoughts from any bitterness or anger that I may still be carrying around.

I ask that You allow me to move forward with grace and dignity. In Your name.

Amen.

A PRAYER FOR GRATITUDE

Lord,

Your blessings in my life are so many, especially during my hardest times. Thank You for having placed so many families and friends around me who supported me. I will always focus on all the good and place all my indebtedness in You while I look forward to all the provisions You have for me in the future.

Amen.

When we focus our minds on God, we will become stronger in our faith. We have to make up our minds to pray constantly while never losing hope. As it is written in *1 Thessalonians 5:17* (KJV), "Pray without ceasing." As Christians, we must grasp a good understanding of the Bible. "Hunger and thirst" should be our "motto" as we further our walk with Him.

We also have to speak about God's goodness to others, especially to those who ask us questions.

It is said that the Bible is the most-read book in the world. So I ask, How come we don't go to it regularly? Some think that it's very complicated and difficult to understand. This is where prayer intercedes and we can get some clarity.

This book is full of knowledge. Don't fret. The Holy Spirit will channel all your needs to understand it. *Luke 24:44* (KJV) clearly states, "And he said unto them, Those spoke unto you, while I was yet with you, that all things must be fulfilled, which when written in the law of Moses, and in the Psalms concerning me."

The Bible was not written for a selected few; it's for each one of us. It explains in detail how we all can be saved. Nothing in this world gives us an understanding like the Word of God. Indulging in it allows us to see all the goodness He has stored up for us.

The oil baron drilling off the coast will eventually find oil. We, too, should aspire to have a deeper drive to soak up the word.

How beautiful it is to sit alongside a stream and watch the water meander over rocks! Sometimes there are obstacles, but it never stops flowing. So just like the stream and the oil baron, we also must be driven. We must have a purpose.

Paul reminds us in *1 Corinthians 7:24* (KJV), "Brethren, let everyman, where he is called there, abide with God." We all must carry ourselves in a manner pleasing to Him.

We must do our spiritual exercises. Help others without looking for anything in return. Most of us live our lives in disobedience to our Lord and Savior, trying to hold onto things that are way out of our grasp. We also put a huge gap between ourselves and God. But He is there to restore any severed relationship we may have with Him. We all have to take into account that life, death, and the resurrection of Jesus (God in the flesh) will always make possible a new life with Him.

Some don't believe that God exists because they can't see Him, but they have to remember what *2 Corinthians 5:7* (KJV) says: "For we walk by faith, not sight."

CONCLUSION

As I conclude my book, my only hope is that you have been inspired to deepen your faith in God. Keep in mind that faith is not a set of beliefs or doctrines but a very strong relationship with God—a God Who loves and will very much like a relationship with you. Even though at times we become broken, as crayons sometimes do, they still color.

We are resilient.

This world we are living in is full of trials, difficulties, and doubt, so we must remember that the living God is always beside us and that He is working all things together for our good, as stated in *Romans 8:28* (KJV), "And we know that all things work together for good to them that love God, to them who are called according to his purpose." Let's continue to walk by faith and not by sight, and to always cling to His goodness, mercy, and grace. We must have a deeper understanding of Him and always keep our hearts open to accept His love.

Our hope in God must be shared with those around us so that they may also come to know His abiding love. It's written in *Psalm 34:8* (KJV), "O taste and see that the Lord is good: blessed is the man that trusteth him."

May the Lord bless you and keep you, and may His face shine upon you and give you grace.

A CONCLUDING PRAYER

Dear God,

As I come to the end of my book, I thank You for your unselfish gift of faith and for remaining in my life. I want to thank You for the numerous ways that You have revealed Yourself to me and for all Your love, grace, and mercy.

I pray for anyone who reads my book. I want them to be inspired as they continue their walk with You so that they experience the richness of Your love, as I have.

Lord, I ask that You strengthen our faith and help us see all that You can do. When we are struggling with doubt, show us Your power. May we always know the truth of Your Word and the reality of Your precious love.

Finally, may we glorify Your name in everything that we do.

I am asking these things in Your name.

Amen.

> And if it seems evil unto you to serve the Lord, choose you this day whom you will serve; whether the gods which your fathers served that were on the other side of the flood, or the gods of the Amorites, in whose land ye dwell: *but as for me and my house, we will serve the* L*ORD*. *(Joshua 24:15)*

Thank You.

NOTES

NOTES

NOTES

NOTES

ABOUT THE AUTHOR

As an unwavering Christian believer, Judith Jennifer is honored to present this book of her profound journey with God. She draws from her experiences and her deep commitment to faith. She embarked on this journey with a passionate desire to help you understand the deep power of trust. Her heart is grounded in God's love, and she wants to help others navigate life's uncertainties. She prays that the words she writes will resonate deeply, as they encourage you to embrace trust as an anchor in your own spiritual journey. May this book help guide you to the boundless rewards that await as you place all your trust in God.

Printed in the USA
CPSIA information can be obtained
at www.ICGtesting.com
CBHW040233231024
16239CB00062B/991